This book is dedicated to my teacher, Mrs. Johnson.

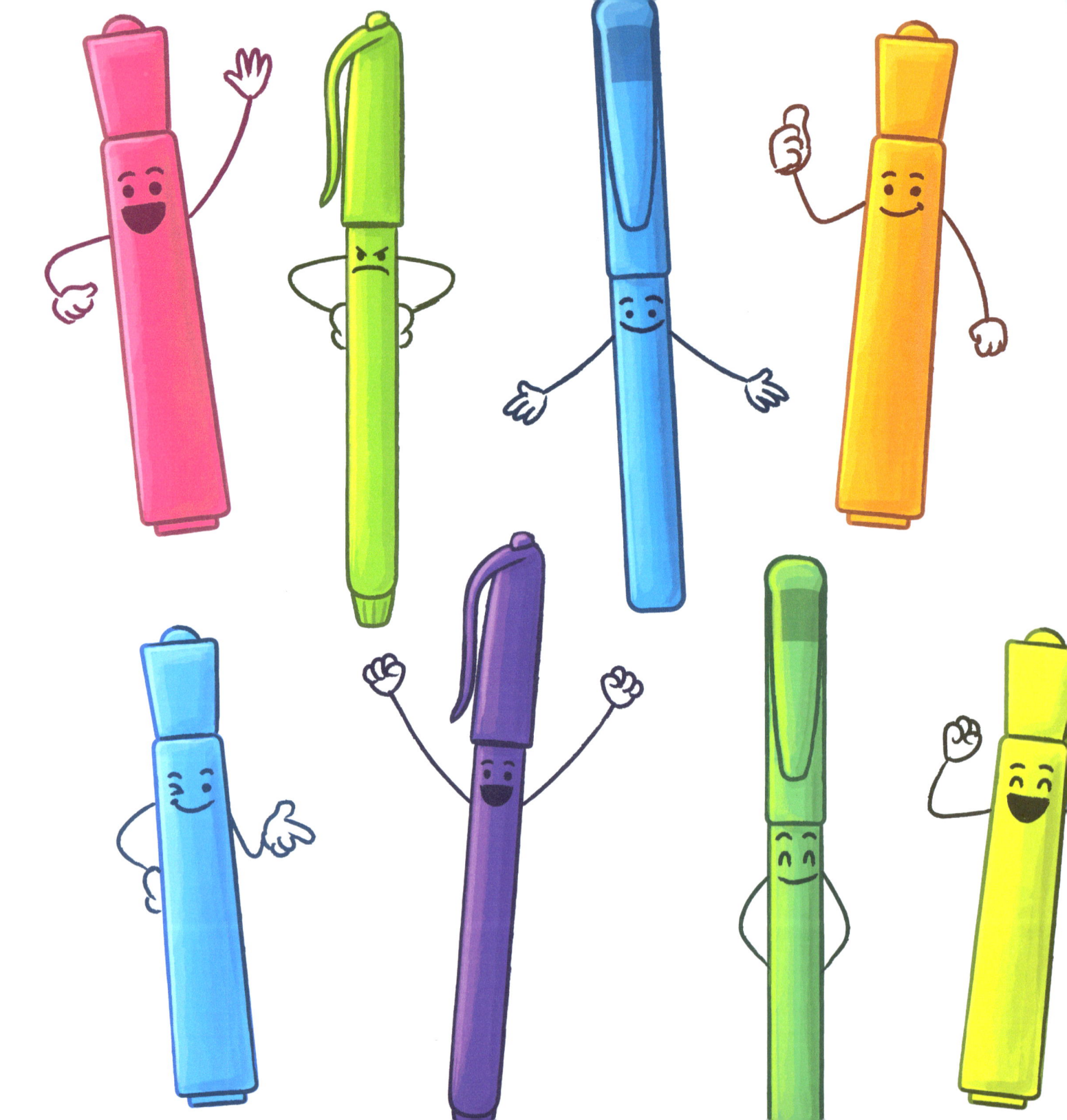

Copyright © 2023 Jennifer Jones
All copyright laws and rights reserved. Published in the U.S.A.
For more information, email info@ninjalifehacks.tv
Paperback ISBN: 978-1-63731-818-8   Hardcover ISBN: 978-1-63731-820-1
eBook ISBN: 978-1-63731-819-5

Find the Highlighters on Strike lesson plans at ninjalifehacks.tv

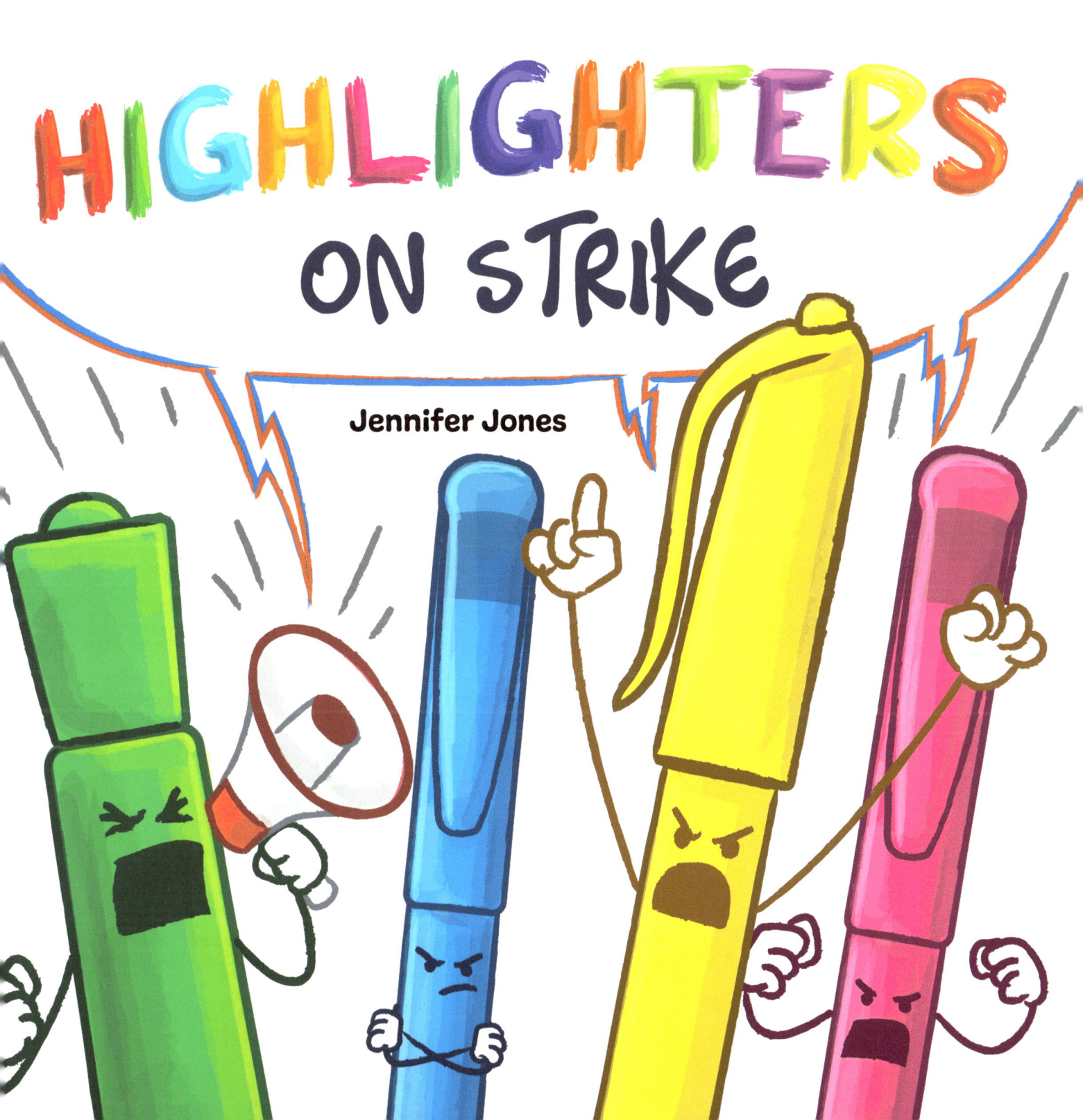

When words on a page of paper
simply just don't feel enough,
we swoop right in with yellow ink
to brighten the black and white up.

When you need to see what's important,
we make it crystal clear.
So you'd think the users would be gentle,
especially when we're near.

They try to bend and snap our bodies.
Or WORSE they chew our ends.
They giggle and proudly show our mangled plastic
to all their school friends.

In big, bold yellow letters, we wrote about what we didn't like. "THAT'S IT, WE'VE HAD ENOUGH," we wrote. "THE HIGHLIGHTERS ARE GOING ON STRIKE!"

Until then, they'd have to see pages
of only white and black.
Some things would have to change
if they ever wanted us back.

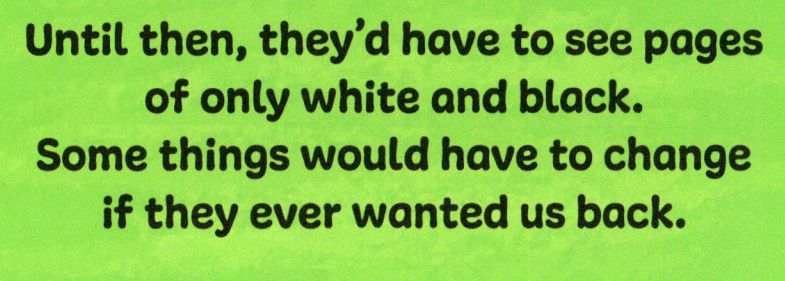

Then they gathered in a huddle
and grabbed some paper for a reply.
"We're sorry we hurt you," they said.
"We'll make it up to you. Please let us try."

"We won't let your ink dry out.
We'll remember to put back your tops.
We'll make sure to place you back carefully
and make sure all the abuse stops."

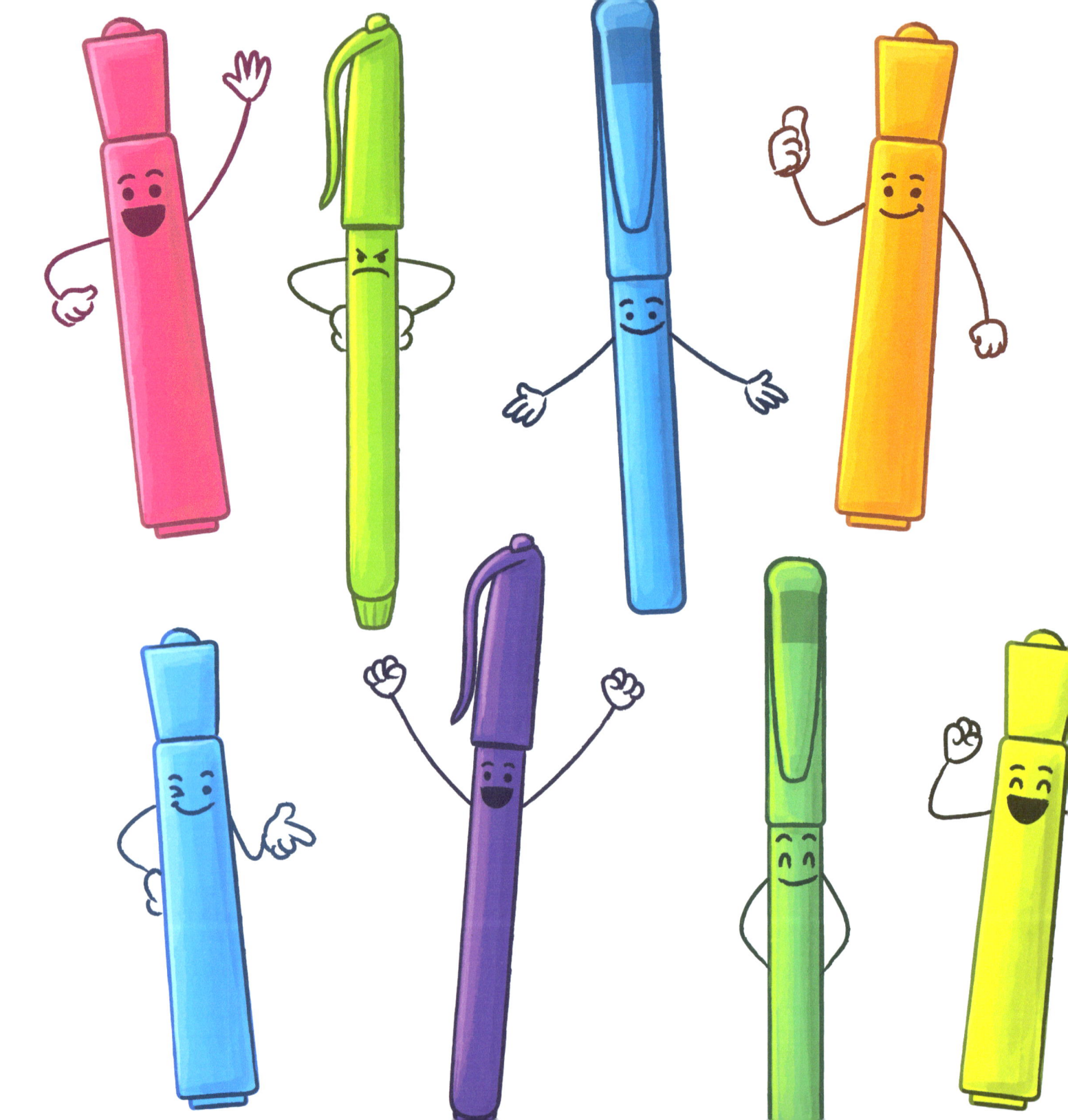

www.ingramcontent.com/pod-product-compliance
Lightning Source LLC
Chambersburg PA
CBHW041523070526
44585CB00002B/53